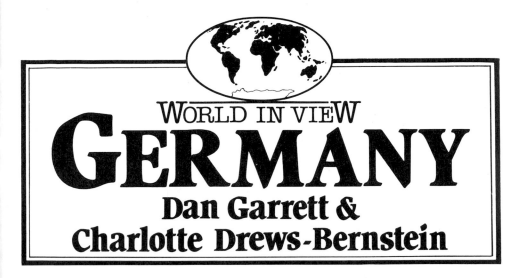

WORLD IN VIEW
GERMANY
Dan Garrett &
Charlotte Drews-Bernstein

HEINEMANN CHILDREN'S REFERENCE
a division of Heinemann Educational Books Ltd
Halley Court, Jordan Hill, Oxford OX2 8EJ

OXFORD LONDON EDINBURGH
MELBOURNE SYDNEY AUCKLAND
MADRID ATHENS BOLOGNA
SINGAPORE IBADAN NAIROBI HARARE
GABORONE KINGSTON PORTSMOUTH NH(USA)

ISBN 0 431 00444 7

A CIP catalogue record for this book
is available from the British Library

© Heinemann Educational Books Ltd 1991
First published 1991

Designed by Julian Holland Publishing Ltd

Printed in Hong Kong

90 91 92 93 94 95 10 9 8 7 6 5 4 3 2 1

Acknowledgements

We would like to thank the many people who have helped us with this book, in particular, in Germany, Christiane Rodmann, Professor Wolfgang Stützer, and many friends in Leipzig and Dresden. In Britain, Bob Dixon, Ingrid Hassler and Geoff Sherlock have made many valuable suggestions. Officially we were enemies 50 years ago. We were children when our two countries were fighting each other. Now we are friends, and this book is the result.

Photo credits: Cover J. Allan Cash; title page D. Garrett, 8, 9 G. Sherlock, 10 D. Garrett, 11, 12 G. Sherlock, 13, 14, 16, 19 D. Garrett, 23 Hulton-Deutsch, 26 Associated Press Photo, 28 J. Allan Cash, 32 G. Sherlock, 33 J. Allan Cash, 35 Associated Press Photo, 40 D. Garrett, 41 G. Sherlock, 42 D. Garrett, 43 Reuben Garrett, 46 G. Sherlock, 48 D. Garrett, 50, 52, 53 G. Sherlock, 55, 56 D. Garrett, 59, 61 J. Allan Cash, 62 G. Sherlock, 63 J. Allan Cash, 64, 66, 69, 70, 73 D. Garrett, 74 G. Sherlock, 77, 79 D. Garrett, 81, 84, 85 G. Sherlock, 89 D. Garrett, 90 G. Sherlock, 93 D. Garrett.
Cover: *Neuschwanstein Castle, Bavaria*
Title page: *Cologne across the River Rhine*

Although Germany was united in October 1990, there are many economic and cultural differences between the two old states, East and West, that will take several years to change. In order to account for these differences we have kept the use of East and West Germany in this book.

Contents

1 One nation – two states

Few weeks have gone by in recent years without Germany making headlines. Great changes are happening, and these changes are themselves the result of upheavals in German history. A traveller passing through the beautiful German countryside may not be aware of the hidden worries of the people.

Germany was a single country until the end of the Second World War. Then, from 1949 until 1990, Germans had to live in two states, called the Federal Republic of Germany and the German Democratic Republic. The names are usually simplified to West Germany and East Germany. How the German nation came to be split, and what this meant, is told in chapter four.

Deutschland

The German word for Germany is *Deutschland* (pronounced Doych-land).

The German for the Federal Republic of Germany is *Bundesrepublik Deutschland,* or BRD (in English, the FRG, usually known as West Germany).

The German Democratic Republic is *Deutsche Demokratische Republik* in German or DDR (in English, the GDR, usually known as East Germany.

Länder or states of Germany

N

North Sea

DENMARK

Baltic Sea

SCHLESWIG-HOLSTEIN

MECKLENBURG-VORPOMMERN

HAMBURG

BREMEN

POLAND

LOWER SAXONY

BERLIN

NETHERLANDS

BRANDENBURG

NORTH-RHINE-WESTPHALIA

SAXONY-ANHALT

SAXONY

THURINGIA

HESSEN

LUXEMBOURG

RHINELAND-PALATINATE

CZECHOSLOVAKIA

SAARLAND

BAVARIA

BADEN-WÜRTTEMBERG

FRANCE

kilometres

0   80

miles

0   60

SWITZERLAND

AUSTRIA

Sadly, the frontier between the two states has caused much trouble. However, just as two people in a family may argue but still stick together, so Germans in both states continued to feel they belonged to one nation. Now, the two states have been united into a single German Republic.

Connections

East and West Germany were in the middle of Europe and shared borders with many countries. This led to both prosperity and problems. West Germany had frontiers with Denmark, the Netherlands, Belgium, Luxembourg, France, Switzerland and Austria, while East Germany had frontiers with Czechoslovakia and Poland. West Germany had ports on both the North Sea and the Baltic Sea (which Germans call the *Ostsee* – East Sea). East Germany, on the other hand, was almost landlocked. Its only access was to the Baltic Sea. East German ships had to pass through the narrow straits between Sweden and Denmark before reaching the open ocean.

The landscape

The northern half of Germany is flat, gently rolling countryside. This has made it easy to build railways and motorways, so that there are good links with surrounding countries. Further south, there are mountain ranges like the Black Forest (*Schwarzwald*), the Taunus, the Harz and the Erzgebirge. These Central Uplands (as they are called) rise fairly gently from the surrounding countryside. They are not very high — around 600 metres (2000 feet) – but high enough for railways and motorways to avoid them if possible.

The Sieberberg valley is in the Harz mountains. These are the most northerly mountains in Germany. They rise from the northern plains to just over 1100 metres (3600 feet).

The German landscape is rather like a staircase rising from north to south. The lowest step is the northern plain, and the next step is on to the Central Uplands. There is a third step up to the lower Alps, on the borders of Switzerland and Austria. In these two countries there is a fourth step on to the high Alps themselves. The Alps make a huge mountain barrier between central Europe and countries to the south like Italy.

Large rivers flow through Germany. Several of these rivers flow through other countries as well. The Rhine rises in Switzerland and flows north through West Germany into the Netherlands and so to the North Sea. The Elbe rises in Czechoslovakia and flows north-west, first through East Germany and then West Germany to

Sizes and comparisons

Germany occupies a rough rectangle about 750 kilometres north to south by 500 kilometres wide (450 x 300 miles).

The East German part was smaller, covering about 40 per cent of the land area of the West German part.

The West German part had about the same area as Britain, about 50 per cent the area of France or Spain, and about 2.5 per cent of the area of the US.

In 1989, 62 million people lived in West Germany. Nearly 17 million lived in East Germany. For comparison, 56 million were living in Britain and 228 million in th US.

The extreme south of Germany is bordered by the Alps. The narrow valleys provide routes through to Austria and Switzerland. The German Alps are in Bavaria, the largest Land *in Germany.*

Huge barges pass one after another beneath the steep slopes of the Loreley on the middle Rhine. Once, this bend was so dangerous that many boats hit the rocks and sank. A legend grew up that a maiden lured sailors to their destruction.

reach the North Sea beyond Hamburg. The Danube rises in the Black Forest, and flows eastwards through a number of East European states before reaching the USSR and the Black Sea. The great length of these rivers and the way they connect different countries has made them very important for trade. Germany has always been the centre of important trade routes, particularly those from Asia and the Middle East. Many wars have been fought along the borders and these have changed continually. Someone flipping through a book of maps of Germany from 800 to the present would not see the borders as a single unchanging line. Instead they would look like a blur, in some places shifting by hundreds of miles. Sometimes Germany has been much bigger than even today's united Germany. Near the borders, towns, and even cities, have sometimes been German, and sometimes belonged to another country. The city of Gdansk, which is in Poland, was once in Germany with the German name Danzig. The city of Strasbourg and the surrounding province of Alsace have sometimes belonged to Germany, sometimes to France, where they belong today.

Cities and countryside

Germany, is heavily industrialized. Industry in the West German part is concentrated around major cities such as Munich, Hamburg and Stuttgart, and in the area known as the Ruhr. This includes industrial cities such as Essen, Bochum, Düsseldorf and Gelsenkirchen. East German

At Passau, near the Czechoslovakian border, the Inn and Danube rivers meet. These rivers flow eastward out of Germany providing a trade route to the east.

11

industry is mainly concentrated around Leipzig, Karl-Marx-Stadt (*Chemnitz*), Halle and Dresden. There is also a concentration around Berlin.

Germany can be imagined as having two faces. One is of a rolling countryside dotted with small towns and villages. The other is of large modern cities with spiders' webs of power lines, railways and motorways. Fortunately, industry is packed mainly into areas around the large cities. Outside the industrial zones, fields and forests stretch to the horizon, and the country towns are picturesque, sometimes even quaint. In East Germany that quaintness has resulted from a lack

Ludwigshafen on the River Neckar is part of Europe's most heavily industrialized region.

Many small German towns, such as Bacharach, feature fachwerk, *a traditional style of building.*

of resources for modernization and the quaintness is often side by side with drab buildings and peeling paint. In West Germany, any quaintness has lived on in local customs, fairs and festivals, kept alive by people with a home computer in the children's room.

2

From Agrippa to Bismarck

What we know about the first people living in Germany comes mainly from Roman sources. It was the Romans who gave the land the name Germania. Living in Germany were several different peoples, among them the Saxons.

Where the River Mosel joins the Rhine, the Romans set up a frontier outpost. Today, the modern city of Koblenz stands on the same spot, and cruise ships and barges pass where slaves once rowed Roman galleys.

Germania

Two thousand years ago, the Roman Empire had spread out from Italy to northern boundaries marked by the Rhine and Danube rivers. The edges of the Empire were defended by army camps which slowly grew into cities. One of these was

called Colonia Claudia Ara Agrippinensium. Such an awkward name was shortened to its first word, which means 'colony'. Today, Colonia is known as Cologne (*Köln* in German). The centres of many southern German cities are built over the remains of Roman settlements – Koblenz, Trier and Mainz, for example.

From about AD400 many nomadic warrior tribes from Central Asia fought their way westwards. The result of several centuries of upheavals was that Germania became home for many new peoples, particularly Slavs in the east, and Franks in the west.

The Holy Roman Empire

The Franks became one of the strongest peoples, ruling an empire which is roughly where West Germany, Belgium, and France are today. On Christmas Day AD800, the Pope crowned one of the Frankish kings as emperor of this territory in recognition of the wars he had fought against the enemies of Christian Europe. The emperor was Karl der Grosse, kown in French as Charlemagne. When Charlemagne fought the Saxons in north Germany and won, he created a huge Christian empire.

The western half of Charlemagne's empire spoke Frankish, a 'Romance' language, coming originally from the Romans. The eastern half spoke a Germanic language. The halves were split between Charlemagne's sons, and this division led eventually to two separate nations, France and Germany.

The Germany of this time was not a single state. It was a number of 'dukedoms', tiny states ruled

When Charlemagne died, he was honoured with an octagonal chapel built over his tomb. The chapel still stands today as part of Aachen cathedral. Later on, Aachen changed from a central capital to a border town and, because of the many wars fought around it, the city has sometimes been German and sometimes French, under the name Aix-la-Chapelle.

by a duke. In the north was Saxony, in the centre Franconia, while Swabia was in the south-west and Bavaria in the south-east. At that time Switzerland and Austria did not exist, and so Swabia and Bavaria stretched to the high Alps and the natural frontier with Italy. There were other smaller states too. The whole collection of German states had strong trade links with Italy. They also helped the Pope fight crusades against the non-

Christian Turks and Slavs. In AD962, the Pope rewarded the German king, Otto the Great, with the title of emperor. After that, the German states began to be known as the Holy Roman Empire of the Germans. This empire would last until 1806.

Trade and power

In the twelfth and thirteenth centuries, many of the German dukedoms grew rich. Routes were opened up over the Alps and wealth from Italy was used to start metal mining industries and trade with Scandinavia. Great banking empires were created, the best known belonging to the Fugger family in Augsburg. Cities were joining trading leagues at that time and Germany's Hanseatic League was one of the most powerful.

The Hanseatic League

Around 1300, when traders from different German cities went abroad, they were called Hanse meaning 'little group'. They traded across Europe in furs from Russia, corn from eastern Germany and Poland, fish from Scandinavia, wool from England, and wine from France and the Rhineland.

By 1356, over 100 cities had joined into a league of trading groups, the Hanseatic League. Their numbers swelled to 200 at the height of the Hanse's power. The Hanseatic League was extremely powerful, more powerful than some countries. The League had its own ships to fight pirates, and its own army. It even joined with Sweden to fight Denmark. After 1669 the Hanse broke up, but Hamburg, Lübeck and Bremen are still called Hanseatic Cities.

Two quite different causes cut back Germany's power in the sixteenth and seventeenth centuries. Firstly, the Netherlands, Spain and England built up huge colonies which brought them prosperity (while often causing suffering to the native peoples in those colonies).

Secondly, a young Augustinian monk from Saxony started a religious revolution in Wittenberg. The effects of that upheaval are still with us. The monk was Martin Luther.

Luther and Protestantism

In October 1517, Luther nailed 95 'theses', or points, to the door of Wittenberg Cathedral. His list criticized many aspects of the all-powerful Catholic Church. Where the church taught that people were saved by good deeds, Luther claimed they were saved by faith. He also argued that a person could confess to God directly, without this confession having to be heard by a priest. Nor was a priest needed to explain the Bible, which at that time could only be read in Latin. So Luther translated the Bible into German, finishing in 1522.

Luther's teachings began a religious revolution. Ordinary people then took Luther's ideas a stage further. At that time, many people were serfs. Rather like slaves, they each belonged to a nobleman who also owned the land. If Luther said there could be religious freedom, couldn't people also be freed from serfdom? Riots broke out.

Many rulers, too, wanted to become Lutherans in order to break the power of the Pope. At the Diet (or Council) of Speyer, a Catholic majority banned the new reforms. When Luther's

Martin Luther preached his first sermon in the chapel of Hartenfeld Castle on the banks of the River Elbe at Torgau.

followers protested, they were given the name 'protestants'.

Fighting started between Protestants and Catholics, lasting many decades. The worst time was the Thirty Years War, from 1618 to 1648. Germany was left in ruins. Almost unbelievably, war, starvation and disease reduced the population from 21 million to 13 million. It was a disaster. The peace treaty left Germany as a scattering of over 300 tiny states and self-governing cities. Many of them would not equal other European states in prosperity for 250 years. At the same time, France was able to have a strong influence over German affairs, and this lasted through to the Napoleonic wars in the early nineteenth century.

The Habsburg family and the Austro-Hungarian Empire

The Pope usually appointed German emperors, and this annoyed the more powerful German noblemen. In 1355, they set up a new system, with seven top noblemen electing the emperor. After 1438, members of the Habsburg family were regularly made emperor, and the richest and most powerful of these was Charles V. He ruled between 1519 and 1556 and much of his power rested on the wealth created by flourishing German trade. Marriages with other European royal families meant that Habsburgs also ruled in Spain, much of Italy, Austria and Hungary. The Thirty Years War ended the Habsburg's superiority, and the family turned to building up a German empire among the countries along the Danube. This became the powerful Austro-Hungarian Empire.

The 'late' nation

Many of the hundreds of German states found strength by joining together in confederations. By the mid-nineteenth century, the two strongest German states were Austria and Prussia. Austria had its own empire, linked with Hungary. Prussia had grown to a territory stretching from Berlin to Russia, and linked to other western German confederations. In 1866, these two opposing powers fought a war. Finally, Prussia's prime minister, Otto von Bismarck, was able to create a united German state in 1871. However, it did not include Austria, and Austria is still separate today. Far later than most other countries in western Europe, Germany had become a single state. It would last only 74 years.

3   A European battleground

The pressures that led to the First World War were boiling up at the end of the nineteenth century. Britain was a rich world power and its navy protected its merchant ships as they traded with a global empire. 'We want a place in the sun, too,' said the German emperor, Wilhelm II, and Germany started building up its own navy. Leaders in France and Russia, as well as Britain, built up their own forces in competition.

The First World War

In 1914, there were clashes between some of the small states now forming Yugoslavia. They were tied by a spider's web of treaties and alliances to the great powers, who joined in to help them. Germany and the Austro-Hungarian Empire were on one side. Russia and France were on the other. When Germany marched through Belgium to invade France, Britain joined in to help Belgium. So Germany had enemy forces to east and west.

The armies dug trenches to protect soldiers from machine-gun and rifle fire. Eventually, a double line of trenches stretched from the northern French coast all the way to the Swiss frontier. For four years there were hundreds of battles. Each battle killed tens of thousands of soldiers and won perhaps no more than one kilometre (half a mile) of ground. Attacks 'over the top' between the trenches were stopped by barbed wire and the new machine-guns which could fire bullets continuously.

Britain had to bring troops from its Empire, and in 1917 the US joined in. The European war had become a world war. By 1918, Germany was unable to get supplies and reinforcements, and had to give in. Over eight million people died in the war.

The Weimar Republic

The Allies (Britain and France and the countries on their side) ended the war by making the Germans agree to a peace treaty. The Treaty of Versailles was signed in 1919, and was meant to punish Germany. France took back Alsace and Lorraine, and occupied the Rhineland. Large parts of Prussia were given to Poland, and Germany's few colonies were taken away. The Allies put a limit on the German army and fleet, and banned submarines. Germany also had to repay the Allies with ships, money and goods. Never again, thought the Allies, will Germany be a threat to us. 'Never again' turned out to be 20 years.

By the end of the war Germany's government had lost control. Sailors and workers began a revolution. They set up Worker's Councils in Kiel and Hamburg, while Bavaria proclaimed itself an independent socialist republic. Emperor Wilhelm abdicated, and the Socialist parties took control. At the historic little town of Weimar, politicians met in February 1919 and formed a republic. Berlin would continue to be the capital of the new 'Weimar Republic'.

There were extreme differences between some

Inflation in the Weimar Republic

The mark is Germany's unit of currency, like the British pound or the American dollar. During the Weimar Republic the value of the mark fell drastically.

In October 1921, a German needed 181 marks to buy one dollar. In July 1922, a German needed 670 marks to buy one dollar. In August 1922, a German needed 4500 marks to buy one dollar. By November 1923, banknotes were totally worthless, and had to be replaced with completely new money.

After the First World War, Germany was struck by runaway inflation because the government had to make huge payments to the Allies. The money became increasingly worthless until, by 1923, a single dollar was worth 4200 million marks. Children were allowed to play with piles of money as even the amount shown here had virtually no value.

of the political parties in the Weimar Republic. The Communists, for example, wanted Germany to become a Soviet Republic. Other parties favoured a monarchy, and yet others were totally against democracy. So a struggle began, to sort out the kind of state Germany was to become. The struggle took place in the streets. Revolts, protests and fighting were common. Politicians such as the Communist Rosa Luxemburg were murdered. Had people tried to behave like republicans, and discuss their differences instead of fighting, the Weimar Republic might have survived. Instead, it was 'a republic without republicans.' At the same time, German people could buy less and less for their money. This was because the payments Germany had to make to the Allies helped cause terrible inflation. By 1924 most people's savings would buy next to nothing. It was cheaper to paper walls with banknotes rather than wallpaper!

Hitler's rise to power

Among the many smaller political parties at that time was the very right-wing National Socialist party, the Nazis. Adolf Hitler, their leader, could arouse large crowds with passionate speeches. Other politicians ridiculed him, but many Germans found Hitler strong and convincing. He offered solutions to Germany's problems. He said the Communists were to blame, and the Jews. After the shame and suffering of the Treaty of Versailles, Hitler told people to start feeling proud of being German again.

In 1929, a world economic crisis caused German money (amongst others) to collapse again. Many businesses went down with it. By 1932, six million

---

The Volkswagen
Hitler promised every German family its own car. This was to be the 'Volkswagen' or 'people's car'. The familiar 'Beetle' car is a direct descendant of the first 'Volkswagen', and of course Volkswagen is still the name of the car manufacturer.

---

people had lost their jobs, and families were suffering terrible hunger and misery. When the Nazis put up a poster, 'Hitler – our last hope', people believed it. Growing numbers supported Hitler, and in 1933 he was legally appointed Chancellor, as the head of government was called. He began to put his ideas into action with a vengeance.

Firstly, Hitler completely disbanded all trade unions and political parties. Anyone who opposed Hitler was beaten up, imprisoned or murdered by a private army under Nazi control. Socialists and Communists who hadn't gone into hiding or into exile were rounded up and put into concentration camps. Hitler was now a complete dictator and could make laws as he chose. His state was based on legal terrorism.

Secondly, Hitler ordered the armed forces to expand secretly. Submarines were again built, despite the Allies' ban. The third step took a little longer, but within four years Hitler had created an economic miracle. Businesses prospered, and large public schemes (such as building motorways) created new jobs. By 1937, everyone was employed. For many Germans, living standards had become much better.

The Second World War

Next, Hitler began to expand Germany by taking over Austria (where he was born) and invading Czechoslovakia. Then on 1 September 1939, Hitler ordered the invasion of Poland. France and Britain had previously agreed to help Poland, and two days later they declared war against Germany.

This photograph is of Hitler reviewing the German troops in Warsaw after the invasion of Poland in 1939. This was one more example of Hitler's 'empire building'. He called 'his' Germany the Third Reich. Reich means state or empire. Hitler counted the Holy Roman Empire as the first Reich and Bismarck's unified Germany as the second.

For seven months the Allies did nothing. Then, in a lightning strike, which was known as *Blitzkrieg*, German troops occupied Denmark and Norway. Next was France's turn, and by June 1940 almost all of central Europe was controlled by Hitler. Britain stood alone, only 34 kilometres (21 miles) away from occupied France.

In Germany and the territories occupied by Hitler, a terrible thing was happening. Hitler had always believed that the world owed all its troubles

to the Jews. At the same time, he believed it was German destiny to become the *Herrenvolk*, the Master Race. Now Hitler put his racist ideas into practice. He ordered the total extermination of the Jews. In Germany and the occupied countries, Jews were first made to wear yellow identification stars, the five pointed star of David, and then rounded up and sent to immense concentration camps. The fittest people were used as slave labour in German industry, but almost all were killed. Huge gas chambers were built, which the Nazi guards pretended were shower rooms. As trainloads of Jews arrived, they were made to strip and go into the 'shower rooms' where they were gassed. The bodies were burnt and the gas chambers made ready for the next group. Not only Jews were killed in the concentration camps, but many people from the occupied countries, many gypsies, many homosexuals, and many of Hitler's political opponents, including churchmen.

Anne Frank

The story of one Jew has become world famous. Anne Frank was born in Frankfurt in 1929, the daughter of a Jewish banker. In 1933 the family escaped to Amsterdam and, when the Netherlands were overrun by Germany in 1940, courageous Dutch friends hid the family in a secret room. There they lived safely for four years. Tragically, the family were betrayed, and taken away to be gassed. We only know the story because Anne kept diaries which have since been published. The Anne Frank House is now a museum, commemorating the past and inviting people to fight against racism.

This huge monument on a hillside outside Weimar commemorates the people from many different nations who died in the nearby concentration camp at Buchenwald. The Nazi regime caused the death of millions of people in forced labour and concentration camps.

From 1940, an aerial war was fought between Britain and Germany. The Blitz, as it was called, destroyed a lot of British towns. In return, Britain bombed German cities, so that by the end of the war, Berlin, Hamburg, Dresden and many other cities had been devastated.

The US army, and British and Commonwealth troops, invaded France and Sicily in 1944. In the east, the Soviet Union was repelling the German invasion. So Germany was caught between two huge armies, and cut off from essential supplies. The end was a matter of time. On 25 April 1945, American and Russian troops 'linked hands across the River Elbe' at Torgau. Soon after, Hitler committed suicide in Berlin, and the German forces surrendered on 8 May.

4 Germany divided

Once Germany was defeated, it was split into four zones, occupied by Britain, the US, the Soviet Union and France, 'the four powers'. The city of Berlin was almost in the middle of the Soviet zone. As the capital of pre-war Germany, Berlin was given special status. It was divided into four occupied sectors, rather like Germany itself. To get to their sectors of Berlin, the British, French and US forces had to travel about 160 kilometres (100 miles) across the Soviet zone.

The four powers could not agree on a single way of running the four German zones. Eventually, Britain, the US and France merged their three zones and gave the new large zone a single currency. Angry at the other three powers going their own way, the Soviet Union blocked roads and railways linking the new western zone to Berlin's western sectors. People there might have gone short of food and coal, but an Allied airlift kept them going for nearly a year. Finally the four powers came to an agreement. On 23 May 1949, the merged western zone became the new state of West Germany. Similarly, on 7 October, the

---

The Berlin Airlift 24 June 1948 – 12 May 1949
Bomber planes were brought out of retirement. Day and night for 11 months food and coal were ferried into Berlin, to an amazing total of 1.7 million tonnes. The planes soon got nicknamed 'raisin bombers' because of all the dried fruit they carried.

---

remaining Soviet zone became East Germany.

Berlin remained a divided city. Its three western sectors were merged, and West Berlin's government and laws were closely linked with West Germany's. Vehicles could only reach West Berlin on specially marked routes through East Germany. East Berlin became the capital of East Germany.

Government in West Germany

West Germany chose the small city of Bonn for its new capital. Large buildings now house the Federal Government, but Bonn is still small enough for people to call it, with a smile, the *Bundesdorf*, the Federal Village.

There were five parties in the Federal Parliament: the Social Democrats, two Christian Democrat parties who work together, the Liberals ('Free Democrats'), and the Greens. The Greens have only been in Parliament since 1983 when they won votes for their policies which were friendly to the environment.

West Germany was divided into 11 separate states or 'Länder', each with its own parliament. This emphasis on regional government has helped prevent wealth and resources being sucked away into a central capital city. Recently an extreme right-wing party, the Republicans, gained votes in the Länder, but not in the Federal Parliament.

The Chancellor is the most powerful person in government, rather like Britain's Prime Minister. There is also a President who in many ways is only a figurehead. In 1990, the Federal President was Richard von Weizsäcker, and the Federal Chancellor was Helmut Kohl.

Government in East Germany up to 1989
For 40 years, East Germany was centrally governed. The Constitution guaranteed that leadership was always in the hands of the Socialist Unity Party. A State Council with a chairman and 21 members made policy. Separate councils ran the economy and defence.

Until 1989, the 'People's Chamber', or Parliament, had 500 deputies. At election time, people had to vote for a complete list of local deputies. They couldn't vote for a particular candidate or party, nor could they vote in secret. No matter how many votes the different parties and organizations got, they had a fixed number of seats. Really, people had little say in choosing a government.

During the 1970s and 1980s, the most powerful man was Erich Honecker, who was Chairman of the State Council, Chairman of the Defence Council and Secretary of the Socialist Unity Party's Steering Group ('Politburo').

How the two systems developed

The systems in West Germany, and in East Germany until 1989, reflected the differences between the USSR and the other Allies. East Germany was modelled on Soviet lines. Step by step through the 1950s, it became a socialist country. It was also much the poorer of the two German states, for a number of reasons. Not only was it smaller than West Germany, but it had to give the USSR nearly a half of its factory machinery as repayments for losses suffered during the Second World War. In 1953, some of the leadership's decisions over wages led to strikes

After the Second World War, Germany was divided into four zones. Britain, the US and France merged their three zones but the Soviet Union kept its zone separate. The border was once marked by barbed wire and look-out posts. However, in the years, just before 1989, striped posts and small notices were used.

and demonstrations. These were stopped by the East German government with the help of Soviet tanks, but people had lost faith in their leaders.

West Germany became a western-style democracy. Within 15 years of the Second World War ending, West Germany was a rich country again. This happened because of the existing skilled workforce, but also because the US poured aid into West Germany to rebuild cities and re-equip factories.

Trying to live side by side

East Germans began to envy the success of West Germans and many moved to new jobs in West Germany. The 'brain drain' grew larger and larger. By mid 1961, 20 000 people were leaving East Germany each month. The government could not afford to let them go. Barbed-wire fences were put up along the borders, with minefields, sentry towers and guns triggered by tripwires. A heavily-guarded wall was built between east and west Berlin. The Berlin Wall came to symbolize the split between West Germany and East Germany, capitalism and socialism, the US and the USSR.

By sealing itself off from the West, East Germany gave itself the chance to improve things.

The border between East and West Germany was sealed in 1961 and east and west Berlin were divided by a solid, heavily-guarded floodlit wall. This wound through the city between the buildings. On the eastern side a 'no man's land' was created by pulling down or blocking up empty buildings near the wall.

This small country was (until 1990) the most important industrial country of the socialist states, after the Soviet Union. East Germany still kept strong links with West Germany, which became its largest western trading partner.

In West Germany, there were also significant upheavals. In 1968, German students took the main part in huge demonstrations. The students were 'an opposition outside parliament', calling for the parliamentary opposition to be more effective. Out of this student movement came both a terrorist group (the Red Army Faction) and – more long-lasting – a shift of attitudes which later enabled the Green Party to grow.

Life was still irritating for East Germans. Shops were often out of stock, so that a person might have to go on a long and fruitless hunt before finding such everyday items as building sand or car spares. Yet newspapers painted a rosy picture of life. People felt treated like little children, saying, 'put the truth in the newspapers and fresh vegetables in the shops.'

Although travel to other socialist countries was allowed, travel to the West was impossible for most people, except sports personalities, famous artists, politicians, some businessmen and pensioners. Then, after East Germany signed the Helsinki agreement, people were allowed to apply for an emigration permit. In 1984, for example, 35 000 left legally. However, people applying for emigration visas lost their jobs, and the security police pressurized them and their families. Even after years of waiting, the visa might be refused.

All these restrictions made East Germans increasingly angry. When Hungary took down its

Excited East German citizens cross the Glienicker bridge to visit West Berlin after the border was opened in November 1989. During the previous 28 years the bridge was often the site for East-West spy swaps.

border fence with Austria in 1989, it was like a dam bursting. Huge numbers of people flooded out – 344 000 or two per cent of the population during 1989 alone. Finally, in East Germany's 'October Revolution' of 1989, wide-scale protests and the emigration of many skilled workers forced Honecker's downfall. He, his ministers, and many civil servants, were arrested and charged with corruption and misusing their power.

The new interim (temporary) government knew that East Germany could not afford to go on losing so many skilled people. They ended travel restrictions, hoping that people who could visit the West freely wouldn't mind going on living in East Germany. On the night of 9 November, East

Germany opened its border with West Germany, and the checkpoints in the Berlin Wall. In the next few days, 1.5 million East German sightseers poured into West Berlin, joyful and bewildered. Although they returned home, more than 2000 people a day continued to leave East Germany in the next few months. Three million more were estimated to be ready to leave. 'If the West German mark doesn't come to us, we'll go to it in the West,' they said.

The People's Chamber ended the leading role of the Socialist Unity Party, paving the way for genuinely free elections in March 1990. The number of seats was reduced to 400, and many new parties were started to contest them. Some of the parties received West German campaign money. The election resulted in a victory for the centre and centre-right parties, particularly the CDU, the Christian Democratic Union. The Socialist Unity Party vote was massively reduced. As a result, in July the monetary system of East and West Germany were unified and in September, the four allies, France, USA, Britain and USSR signed the treaty of unification which became effective in October. A peaceful revolution had taken place, part of the great upheavals changing all of Eastern Europe.

5   Industry from science

Germany was one of the first countries after Britain to industrialize. Good quality coal and iron ore in the Ruhr and Saarland formed the basis of huge iron and steel combines. Huge finds of rock salt and potash led to large-scale chemical industries. By 1900, Germany rivalled Britain as a great industrial nation.

After division in 1949, both German states became leading industrial nations with a strong export trade. However, industry was organized on quite different lines in the two states. In West Germany there is capitalism. In East Germany, industry had been run on communist lines. These two kinds of economy have led to distinct differences in many other aspects of life.

In both economies, the machine-tool, motor vehicle and chemical industries are the most important. In West Germany, a workforce approaching one million people makes over four million cars and 300 000 trucks and buses each year. This output makes West Germany the third largest vehicle producer after the US and Japan. With 60 per cent of cars exported, Volkswagen, Audi, Mercedes, BMW and Opel are equally well-known outside West Germany. Audi's slogan, '*Vorsprung durch Technik*', 'In the lead through technology', seems to speak for all West German car makers.

East Germany is now changing towards a 'market economy with responsibility for social and ecological care.' Private enterprises are to be favoured against state enterprises, and industry

Capitalism

The capitalist system is often called a market economy. West German businesses from the little corner shop to immense combines like Daimler-Benz are all privately owned. Any people with enough money can set up a business, or buy a share in one. If they are lucky, the business will make money, a profit. If they are unlucky, it will make a loss.

Of course, businesses need to employ people to do the work. The danger with capitalism is that it exploits employees in order to make a profit. Employees may get very low wages or have to work long hours in poor conditions. Owners can choose to shut a business down, throwing their employees out of work. Owners may even transfer to another country where material or labour is cheaper.

Laws are needed to keep capitalism under control, and effective trade unions are needed to ensure the rights of employees. West Germans have strong laws and call their form of capitalism a 'social market economy'.

will no longer be heavily subsidized. The problem for East Germany, though, is that it must become competitive like other market economies. If the factories fail to sell goods, they won't earn the money to pay their workers' wages. Unemployment could reach high levels. One example is the Trabant factory. Their single car model is outdated and its quality is poor. To survive, a high-value modern model is needed, requiring an expensive new production line and a newly trained workforce. A link-up with Volkswagen may provide the much-needed

Communism
The Communist system is often called a planned socialist economy. In East Germany, at least until 1989, all businesses from the corner shop to large-scale enterprises, like the Leuna Chemical Combine, were owned and run by the state or people's co-operatives. This was to prevent employees being exploited. Everyone of working age had a job and wage levels were guaranteed. Wages were often low but planners set costs like food and housing at a low level.

In Communist systems generally, business risks are taken by the state, not by individuals. There is planning, not competition. Industries do not fail, throwing whole communities out of work. The danger is that such state-run enterprises are often poor at matching output to people's needs. There are gluts and shortages. Also, the combines may have to employ more people than they really need. Machinery is often out-of-date, and planners in distant, centralized offices ignore local needs.

technical know-how and the money for buying new plant.

Science and technology

Germany has produced many fine scientists. They seem to excel both in theoretical science and in developing practical applications. August Otto invented the gas engine, and Rudolf Diesel the engine named after him. Karl Benz and Gottfried Daimler both independently developed petrol-driven cars in 1885, and laid the foundations of the modern car industry.

Every other car in East Germany seems to be the 'Trabi', the home produced Trabant with a 600cc, two-cylinder, two-stroke engine. It is a cheaply produced utility car with much of the bodywork made in plastic.

Fritz Haber won a Nobel Prize in 1918 for his process which converts nitrogen from the atmosphere into nitrate for fertilizer. Haber's invention became the basis for the German fertilizer industry. Heinrich Hertz was the first to investigate radio frequencies. Wilhelm Röntgen discovered X-rays and won the first Nobel Prize for physics in 1901.

Wernher von Braun developed Hitler's V1 and V2 missiles as 'vengeance weapons' against Britain in the Second World War. The V1 was a pilotless jet aircraft and the V2 was the first rocket which could travel hundreds of miles in a controlled way. Both carried explosives and were used to bomb

British cities. When the Americans captured Braun and his team in 1945, he went to work in the US. His know-how led to today's intercontinental missiles and moon rockets.

German theoretical scientists won 31 Nobel Prizes between 1901 and 1933 against the US's six. Albert Einstein developed the revolutionary Theory of Relativity, while Max Planck and Werner Heisenberg developed new atomic theories. The work of all three made nuclear power and nuclear bombs possible.

Hitler's persecution of the Jews caused many brilliant scientists, including Einstein to emigrate. This left German science lagging behind and it has still not fully recovered.

Power

Germany has few natural power sources. True, there are large reserves of black coal in western

Immense machines like spidery dinosaurs scoop out brown coal with huge bucket wheels on their front jib. In the German landscape of farms and villages these machines are overwhelmingly ugly. They leave behind great depressions that look like pitted lunar landscapes.

There are 26 nuclear power stations in Germany but there is very strong opposition to their use. They are mainly situated on rivers and there are fears that the cooling water drawn from the rivers could become contaminated with radioactivity.

Germany, but the deep mines make this an expensive energy source. Brown coal is much cheaper to mine because it lies near the surface. Both regions dig brown coal, but East Germany has needed it most, having had almost no other fuel sources of its own. East German output of brown coal is a quarter of the whole world's.

West Germany can supply one quarter of its own natural gas needs, but the rest comes through pipelines from the Netherlands, Norway and the Soviet Union. Both East and West Germany import gas through a 6000 kilometre (4000 mile) pipeline from the Ural mountains in the USSR. East Germany could ill afford to do this, but it had one economic advantage over West Germany, which was a small supply of uranium for nuclear power stations.

Nuclear power is used throughout Germany. There are 21 nuclear power stations in operation in West Germany. East Germany has only five, with one thought to be unsafe. Many riverside sites have been chosen, because the only sea-coasts are in the north. As a result there is a danger of cooling water contaminating these rivers. Ten nuclear power stations use the Rhine, and a radiation leak would be disastrous for Belgium and the Netherlands, besides Germany. People's fears are so strong that nuclear power may be phased out in the future.

Pollution

Pollution is a serious problem in Germany. Not only are the large industries to blame, but also car exhausts, aircraft and home heating. In particular,

This huge chemical works at Espenhain in East Germany has caused so much pollution that the health of people nearby seems to be affected. Local protests have been started to make the works cut down on the pollution in its smoke and steam.

burning brown coal creates very bad sulphuric acid pollution. West Germany recently spent a great deal of money to clean up acid smoke. East Germany has lagged far behind, because of the expense, and along with Poland, Czechoslovakia and Britain, is one of Europe's worst polluters. More pollution comes from the many chemical plants. This has been extremely bad in East Germany, and has probably caused sickness in several areas.

Fortunately, the Green Party is changing people's attitudes. Large numbers of car drivers are changing to lead-free petrol, and manufacturers are turning to environmentally-friendly products. As part of unification West Germany promised financial help to clean up East German pollution, but experts fear it will cost at least two billion marks. A united Germany should make Europe a much cleaner place.

6

From peasant farms to lakes of wine

German farmers are fortunate for their country has a temperate climate. Even so, there are marked variations in the climate.

In the north-west, the closeness of the Atlantic Ocean brings rain regularly throughout the year. Generally, though, summers are moderately warm, averaging about 18°C (64°F) in July. Winters are mild, with January temperatures averaging 1–2°C. (35°F). Further from the Atlantic, the east and the south tend to have rather hotter summers and colder winters. For example , on the north-west coast near the Netherlands, there are about 36 weeks on average between the last frosts of spring and the first frosts of autumn. Around Berlin, there are only 29 weeks, something farmers have to take into account when planning what to grow.

The mountains of the Central Uplands cause large local variations in the weather. On the western slopes, westerly winds coming from the Atlantic full of moisture can cause rainfall of up to 2000 millimetres (80 inches) in a year. On the eastern sides of the mountains, there can be as little as 500 millimetres (20 inches) in a year.

Farms in West Germany
Well into this century, agriculture in Germany was based on small peasant farms clustered around villages. Since the Second World War, though, change has been rapid. In West Germany, many

The flat plains of northern Germany have many large farms. Since the 1950s, thousands of traditional smaller farms have been taken over and now, with modern equipment larger fields are common. This potato field is near Brunswick.

small farms became less and less profitable, and since 1950 three-quarters of those working in agriculture have left for other jobs. Tiny farms have been added to larger ones, so that there are now more than a million fewer small farms. Those that are left are usually run as a sideline. Large farms, though, are an important part of West Germany's capitalist (or market) economy.

Hard though these changes must have been for many country people, they have caused greatly increased productivity. In 1950, one farmer could produce the food for ten people, today he can produce enough for 70. Mostly, farming is mixed, but dairy farming is concentrated in the north-west, in the flatter, wetter lands next to Belgium and the Netherlands. Wheat, sugar-beet and rape for the margarine industry are grown everywhere. In the south, fields of brilliant yellow sunflowers and maize (sweetcorn) are also common.

Farms in East Germany

In East Germany, the numbers of people working on the land also fell steeply after the Second World War, and farms grew larger. These changes didn't go as far as in West Germany, though. The more important change was in farm organization. As with industry, this was centrally planned by the government, at least until 1989. The policy was for farms to be in public ownership, with two main types. There were large nationalized Peoples' Farms, where land and equipment belonged to the state and the farmworkers were state employees. Small co-operatives, however, were much more common and continue to exist. In these, the land was usually owned partly by the state and partly by members of the co-operative. Members owned the farm machinery and vehicles as well. Twenty per cent of income was shared according to land ownership, and 80 per cent according to how much each member had worked. Most members liked working co-operatively, but they now have to face competition with other farmers in the European Community.

Travellers through Germany see huge fields, each with a single crop – cabbage, beans, wheat, for example. This system is called monoculture. In the years before 1989, East Germany developed meat production combines, not unlike western battery farms. All over Germany, modern farming methods have damaged the environment, as they have in other countries. Nitrate fertilizer ends up polluting streams, rivers and eventually the sea. In some areas German farmers have gone back to traditional methods of mixed farming. These organic farms cause much less environmental damage, but may not produce as much food.

Wine growing

The wine-loving Romans probably introduced the grape vine into Germany. In the south, there are some ideal sites, particularly on south-facing slopes. In western Germany, vines crowd up the steep valley sides of the Rhine, the Neckar and the Mosel. Grapes for red wines usually need more sun, and so German vineyards have tended to specialize in white wines, especially those made from Riesling grapes.

Only the extreme south of eastern Germany is

Along the valleys of the Rhine, the Neckar and the Mosel, there are numerous vineyards. This vineyard is at Leutesdorf on the middle Rhine. The crop is harvested in the autumn and by August the grapes are already swelling.

suitable for wine-growing. Commercial vineyards in this region are a low priority, but now people are planting vines along the banks of the Elbe near Dresden.

The European Community

West Germany was a founder member of the European Community (the 'Common Market'). A united Germany has brought East Germany into the Community as well. One of the Community's functions has been to give subsidies to farmers in some countries to help them compete against others. In West Germany, subsidies have gone to dairy farmers in particular. This is because they haven't been able to compete with the more efficient Danes, Dutch and British. Unfortunately, these and other subsidies have led to overproduction. Huge quantities of produce, the so-called butter mountains and wine and milk lakes, have choked warehouses and stores. Members of the European Community are now given quotas (an order saying how much of these things they should produce). As a result, many small farms have gone out of business, or switched to other kinds of farming. Some farmers argue that farming patterns have been badly distorted by the demands of the European Community.

Forestry

Huge forests cover nearly a third of Germany, particularly forests of pine trees. The Black Forest in the south-west, for example, is so-called because the pine trees make a thick cover which blocks out the sunlight. Even at midday, it is dark walking between the trees. The Thüringer Wald

The Germans are very proud of their countryside and the 5.3 million hectares (204 633 square miles) of forests, which are still home to a range of wild animals. Unfortunately, acid rain has caused immense damage to these forests in recent years, threatening the habitat of these animals.

and the Harz are also well-known forests.

Germans love their forests. They are important for recreation, and there are wildlife reserves and well-marked hiking routes (*Wanderwege*). The large forests, particularly in hilly areas, still offer a home to unusual wild animals such as boars, lynx and wild cats. In the lower Alps are ibex, and chamois goats (a type of antelope), as well as the golden eagle.

Sadly, the trees are having a hard time. Acid rain caused by pollution affects trees badly. As a result, about half the trees in both German states are sick or dying. This 'dying of the forests' has been one of the influences on the growing numbers of people voting for the Green Party.

7

From Hannibal's elephants to jets

Germany has always had good connections with neighbouring states. Now, with the unification of Germany, the old transport links between the East and West are being re-opened and improved. Nowhere is this more obvious than in Berlin. Here, underground trains from the city's west have to travel part of the way under east Berlin. They used to go non-stop through 'ghost' stations. Since travel restrictions have been lifted, the re-opened road and rail links are making Berlin a single city again.

Rivers and canals

From earliest times, Germany's rivers have been important for carrying goods. Today, parts of the Rhine are like a water motorway, with huge barges passing every minute or two. They are often so heavily loaded with minerals or metal scrap that the water rushes over the narrow side decks and the barges seem close to sinking.

Another important river for trade is the Elbe, linking West and East Germany and giving access to Czechoslovakia. The huge inland port of Hamburg is 110 kilometres (69 miles) from the mouth of the Elbe. Hamburg is Germany's largest port. It handled 59 million tonnes of goods in 1988. The largest port that was in East Germany is Rostock, on the Baltic Sea. Rostock handles about one-third of Hamburg's tonnage.

A good canal system has been added to the

Hamburg specializes in container shipping. The docks have large cranes capable of unloading ships in hours rather than days. The large number of containers handled each year make Hamburg one of Europe's main ports.

German rivers. Canals are wide, the barges large, and the annual tonnage high. Germany's inland waterway system, the rivers and canals, carries about a quarter of all the country's goods. Ships leaving German ports on the Baltic such as Lübeck and Kiel used to face a long journey around Denmark. In 1919, the Kiel canal (in German, the Nord-Ostsee-Kanal) was opened, dramatically cutting the journey time. Ships up to 40 metres (133 feet) wide can cut across the 99 kilometres (62 miles) between the Baltic and North seas.

Railways

Germany made an early start in building railways. The first line of real importance opened between Dresden and Leipzig in 1839. As German industry

The Jochenstein-Danube canal, near Passau, is part of the network of canals in Germany that have allowed the country to develop such an effective inland waterway system.

grew in the second half of the nineteenth century, so did the railway network serving it.

In the north, the gently rolling plain made it easy for engineers to lay railways across Germany and into neighbouring countries. In the south, the Alps were for many years a formidable barrier. Little had changed since 218BC when the Carthaginian general Hannibal used elephants to pull his army's supplies over the Alpine passes to fight against the Romans. In the late nineteenth century, railway gangs struggled to cut through the very hard rock. With picks, shovels, dynamite and pneumatic drills, they hammered forward, sometimes at only 2.5 centimetres (an inch) an hour. For Germany, the important tunnels were under the St Gotthard and Brenner passes from

Switzerland and Austria into Italy. Today, it is easy to get on a train at Cologne and go straight through to Rome or Athens.

The railway systems in Germany are state-owned and heavily subsidized. They are important carriers of bulk freight. In West Germany, the railways have been modernized to compete against road traffic. Two railways run down either side of the Rhine, for example, and every few minutes a fast train goes by, a passenger express or a long goods train with up to 50 wagons. The railways take some of the pressure off the motorway systems. Since the reopening of the border, the East and West German railway systems are co-operating with each other.

Many country stations in West Germany have been closed to save money. In East Germany local stations were kept open and fares kept low for social reasons. There are still several steam railways. The Harz mountain railway, for example, is worked by sturdy little engines on the narrow metre-gauge. Raising East German railways to West German standards could cost one billion marks.

Roads
Both German states developed large motorway networks. This has been made easier because motorways were started in the 1930s; they were really a German invention. The high unemployment at that time needed a solution, and Hitler started a programme of road-building, using out-of-work labourers. The new roads would also prove useful to Germany's economic development.

Germany has had an excellent network of good roads. These roads have been continuously improved and the Köhlbrand bridge, which carries motor traffic over the Rhine at Hamburg, is a good example of German road engineering. It is over 3940 metres (13 050 feet) long.

In length of motorways, West Germany is second only to the US. Usually there is no motorway speed limit in West Germany, and most people drive around 130 kph (80 mph). In the outer lane, though, cars frequently travel at 160 kph (100 mph) with queues of BMWs and Mercedes all trying to outdo each other. Not surprisingly, accidents are quite common.

On East German motorways, traffic is generally much lighter, except around Berlin and on routes to West Germany. Even so, there is a 100 kph (63 mph) limit. Local roads used to be full of potholes, but they have been much improved in recent years. In both East and West Germany, drivers still quite often find themselves on noisy cobbled roads.

Cologne's strassenbahn or tramway is used by many people because the frequent service does not suffer from traffic jams. In the city centre the tramway runs in the roadway, but this busy tramstop is fenced off.

Membership of the European Community made the border crossing very easy from West Germany into the Netherlands, Belgium and France, for example. Private motorists are often waved through customs and passport checkpoints.

The border crossings in and out of East Germany used to be like small fortresses. Visa and customs restrictions caused long and irritating queues. People were sometimes told to take out all their luggage while the car was searched.

There are tramways in many German cities. Trams are usually two or three coaches joined together, yet they still get full. The frequent service does not suffer from traffic jams. Some cities, such as Hamburg, Munich, Frankfurt and Berlin, have underground train systems.

Air-travel

There are several international airports in West Germany. Frankfurt is the most important. East Germany, with its recent travel restrictions, had only one airport with connections to the west, Schöneberg in East Berlin. Both states had their own airlines: Lufthansa in West Germany, and Interflug in East Germany. Lufthansa is one of the world's larger airlines, and its fleet includes Boeing Jumbos and other wide-bodied jets. Interflug flies Soviet jets. Only since August 1989 has it been possible to fly direct between the two German states.

8   Cities

Berlin was the capital of Bismarck's Germany. When Germany was divided between 1945 and 1990, part of the city belonged to West Germany and part to East Germany. Each half developed a separate character during that time.

West Berlin

West Berlin is a lively city of museums, art galleries and commerce. Modern buildings, by famous architects like Werner Gropius and Aldo Rossi, make the city busy and impressive, but not pretty. The ruined tower of the Gedächtnis Church has been left in the centre of West Berlin as a monument to the Second World War.

The Kurfürstendamm (or ku'damm, as Berliners call it) is the main shopping street. There is even a shopping tower with 14 floors of shops, and of course there are well-known restaurants and cafes

City populations:	
Berlin (west)	1 879 000
Berlin (east)	1 247 000
Hamburg	1 571 000
Munich	1 275 000
Cologne	914 000
Essen	615 000
Frankfurt	592 000
Leipzig	549 000
Dresden	520 000
Karl-Marx-Stadt	313 000
Magdeburg	290 000
Rostock	251 000

The Kurfürstendamm (or Ku'damm as Berliners call it) is the main shopping street of West Berlin. This view is taken from the 22nd floor of the Europa Centre and includes the ruined tower of the Kaiser Wilhelm Memorial Church, kept as a monument to the Second World War.

such as the Kranzler, Kempinski and Möhring.

Berlin is full of *Kneipen*, places to eat and drink, rather like English pubs. They serve special Berlin dishes, such as *Hackepeter* (raw pork with onions), and *Soleier* (pickled eggs). If you are old enough, you can drink Berliner *Weisse*, a light beer with a shot of syrup.

A few important old buildings survive, the elegant Charlottenburg Palace, and the nineteenth century Reichstag which was set on fire in 1933 and heavily damaged in the Second World War. The 'Radio House' (*Haus des Rundfunks*), finished in 1931, was Germany's first broadcasting centre.

Until 1989, one of the biggest tourist sights was also the saddest. At the end of many streets, vehicles and pedestrians were stopped by the Berlin Wall, separating East and West Berlin. On the western side, the wall was daubed with defiant slogans. One of the best was aimed at Erich Honecker, then the East German leader: 'Erich, hand the key over!' On the night of 9 November 1989, people heard the amazing news that border restrictions were lifted. Young and old people climbed on the wall, dancing and singing, laughing and crying. Then East German soldiers began to pull parts of it down. Ordinary people helped, and many Germans took a little piece of the wall home, as a souvenir of a bleak time in their history. Pieces of the wall have gone on sale – even in New York.

Closest to East Berlin is the Kreuzberg district. Squatters have made their homes in seedy alleys running next to streets full of artists' workshops and boutiques selling handsewn silk underwear. In Kreuzberg is the biggest Turkish community outside Turkey. These so-called 'guest-workers' came here with their families after 1961, when the wall prevented East Berliners working in West Berlin.

East Berlin
The most famous of all German streets is here. Unter den Linden, meaning 'under the lime trees' is where people love to stroll and, until 1939, it was fashionable to stop for a meal at one of the elegant restaurants or a drink at one of the cafes. Unter den Linden has been celebrated by German singers such as Marlene Dietrich and writers such as Goethe and Schiller.

At one end of Unter den Linden is the

The Unter den Linden in East Berlin has always been a popular pedestrian area and was made famous in many German songs. It was restored in the 1960s after it had been damaged in the war.

Brandenburger Tor, a massive stone archway under which the German emperor used to enter Berlin. The Nazis made it a centre of their huge flag-waving parades. In 1961, Unter den Linden became a dead end, sealed off beyond the Brandenburg Gate by the Berlin Wall. The Gate was reopened in December 1989 – a historic moment not only for Berliners, but for the whole world.

East Berlin's shopping centre is around Alexanderplatz, where the World Clock shows the time in the different capitals of the world. Prenzlauer Berg is the colourful East Berlin equivalent of Kreuzberg. Younger people are drawn to its alternative lifestyle.

East Berlin is a centre of museums and culture.

The Pergamon Museum houses an altar more than 2000 years old as part of its huge collection. Bertolt Brecht, the famous playwright, returned to Berlin after the war, and founded his own theatre. The Berliner Ensemble still puts on Brecht's plays.

Hamburg

The second largest city of Germany, Hamburg is sober and businesslike. Its shops and houses are imposing rather than colourful. The River Alster (which joins the Elbe at Hamburg) has been widened into two lakes, and in summer they are full of paddle boats, yachts and little passenger ships. The tree-lined banks are a favourite place for sunbathers. In cold winters the Alster freezes over and stalls are set up on the ice to serve skaters and sledgers with hot sausages and Glühwein, a hot mulled wine.

Along the edges of the River Alster at Hamburg, two lakes have been created for the enjoyment of the residents of the city. Elegant houses overlook the parks that border the lakes.

This busy cafe is in the Marienplatz at the heart of Munich, the capital of Bavaria. Eating and drinking are popular pastimes in Munich and it is famous for its beer festival, which takes place in October.

As well as a large port, Hamburg is also important for industry and commerce. More recently it has become a centre for the media. Studio Hamburg produces films, while NDR (Norddeutscher Rundfunk) is the regional radio and television station. Hamburg is also a newspaper and publishing centre.

Munich (München)

Munich is southern and sunny. Where Berlin is hectic, Munich, the capital of Bavaria, has a more relaxed feel. Even so, it's an important business centre, and many international companies have their base there. It is also a city of education and culture with 100 000 students, more publishers than any other German city, and the largest, most modern television and film studios in Europe. Because West Germans found it hard to think of

Bonn as a true capital, they often spoke of Munich as the 'secret capital'.

Leipzig

Leipzig has long been an important industrial centre, producing heavy machinery for the transport, agriculture, and chemical industries. Geographically and historically, Leipzig's situation has made it a trading place between east and west. Leipzig is an important railway centre, and its station is one of the largest in Europe.

Earlier this century Leipzig was internationally famous for its trade fair. With the division of Germany, however, Leipzig lost some of its importance. The new Exhibition Centre is now a bargaining place for trade deals between eastern and western Europe. With East German travel and

The University Square in Leipzig might be made for a city with a much larger population. Even on a sunny day its modern concrete architecture has a bleak feel.

trade restrictions lifted, the Leipzig fair should regain its previous fame.

Leipzig has long been a centre of culture and education, 'a little Paris' as the eighteenth-century writer Goethe called it. For 28 years of his life, the composer Bach was choirmaster at the Church of Saint Thomas. The city was also a centre of the trade union movement with the first German union formed there by Friedrich Lasalle. Lenin published the first edition of the international revolutionary journal *Iskra* in Leipzig in 1900, and it was a centre of resistance to the Nazi movement, commemorated today by a special museum.

In 1989, Leipzig again became a centre of protest. Every Monday evening, people went first to pray, and then to join in street demonstrations against the government. Often, well over 100 000 people took part, many carrying candles to symbolize light in a dark world.

Dresden

Dresden's position on the Elbe made it an early trading centre. Today, it has important electrical industries, and there are a number of specialist Technical Institutes. It was the centre of East Germany's computer technology. Dresden not only has many fine museums, but it is also the home of German opera. The composers Richard Wagner and Richard Strauss were both director's of the Opera House.

On the night of 13/14 February 1945, wave after wave of British and US bomber planes destroyed most of Dresden, killing 35 000 people. The river-front of fine houses, celebrated by the painter Canaletto, had vanished for ever, it seemed.

On the banks of the Elbe, the famous old buildings of Dresden are slowly being restored. Early in the morning, the riverfront again looks like a painting by Canaletto.

Since then, wide new streets and precincts have been carved out of the rubble, and fountains and benches have made the centre of Dresden a pleasant place to stroll. On the banks of the Elbe, the famous old buildings are slowly being restored. The Opera House is complete and looks just as it did when finished in 1878. Many of the churches have been rebuilt, and work has begun on rebuilding the royal palace.

9

Private spending, state spending

The German currency is the mark, divided into 100 pfennig. The German mark is a strong currency, which means it keeps its value well against the other main currencies of the world. German marks can be bought or exchanged easily in other countries.

Between 1945 and 1990, East Germany had its own mark, which could only be used in the socialist countries. Unlike the US dollar or the British pound, the East German mark was not an international currency. During this period, East Germans could not legally buy West German marks. So East Germans found illegal ways of changing money, a 'black market'. However, on this 'black market', people had to pay up to ten East German marks for one West German mark.

One mark again

On 1 July 1990, the two German states set up a monetary union, as a step towards unification. The West German mark became the currency for both states. Everyone in East Germany had to fill out forms with details of all the money they possessed. July 1 was a Sunday, and people could go to their banks and draw West German marks from their accounts. From 2 July, East German marks were worthless. A complicated formula allowed people to exchange part of their money at a rate of one West German mark for each East German mark. The rest had to be exchanged at a poorer rate. In the weeks leading up to the changeover, vans secretly transferred 30 billion West German marks into East German banks. It was a monetary experiment; nothing like it had ever been done before. It was as if all British people had to start using French francs overnight, or Australians suddenly had to use the US dollar. No one knew how it would work in Germany, nor what the final outcome would be.

Standards of living

People have often tried to compare life in the two states. This has been difficult, because of the currency problems, and because life was organized differently. The following monthly budgets of two young couples will give some idea of take-home pay and spending in 1989, a year before monetary union.

Dagmar and Peter live 20 kilometres (12 miles) from the centre of Hamburg in West Germany. Dagmar is a part-time secretary and Peter a car mechanic. In 1989, they took home between them 3600 West German marks per month.

Uta and Ole live in Leipzig. Ole works fulltime as a machine operative in a plastics factory, while Uta is a part-time secretary. In 1989, together they took home about 1328 East German marks per month. This appears a lot less than Dagmar and Peter, and could suggest that East Germans were much poorer. The point, though, is what each couple could actually buy with their money, what their spending power was.

The big difference was in housing. Dagmar and Peter paid 845 West German marks to rent a small two-bedroom centrally-heated apartment. Ole and

Basic vegetables are plentiful enough at this street market in Dresden, East Germany.

Uta had been allocated an old apartment which needed a lot of repairs. It cost only 46 East German marks to rent. Put another way, Dagmar and Peter paid 23 per cent of their income on housing, while Uta and Ole paid only three per cent.

Shopping, food and meals cost Dagmar and Peter 1000 West German marks. That's 23 per cent, nearly a quarter, of their income. The same things cost Uta and Ole 730 East German marks. That's 55 per cent, over half, of their income.

Another quite big difference was that Dagmar and Peter had life insurance which cost 222 West German marks, 6 per cent of their take-home pay. The East German state insured Ole and Peter out of their taxes.

Dagmar went to work by underground train,

while Peter drove to work in a Volkswagen Golf which he was buying with a loan. Their total cost of transport was 700 West German marks, about 18 per cent of their income. Uta had a moped and Ole a secondhand car. Their travel cost 198 East German marks, 14 per cent of their income, and so not very different. Both couples spend about 20 per cent of their income on leisure, clothes and entertainment. The main difference was that Uta and Ole had no telephone, because the waiting list was 12 years at that time.

It's easy to see that in terms of spending power and lifestyles, these two couples were not so very different. The direct comparison between their incomes is misleading.

Many people in West Germany are quite wealthy and can afford to go shopping in expensive shops like this one in Hamburg.

Health and welfare

As part of the 1990 agreement on monetary union, East Germany agreed to a complete change in its social welfare programme. Before 1990, a state-financed insurance scheme paid for health care and sickness benefit. After 1 July 1990, the system became the same as West Germany's, where these costs are met from compulsory insurance schemes. These are paid jointly by employer and employee, so that anyone getting ill in Germany can be sure of treatment. However, in East Germany, people have normally gone to hospitals for treatment. In future, there are likely to be growing numbers of private doctors, dentists and chemist's shops.

Child benefit

East Germany gave very good support to mothers and children. Before 1990, West Germany had been taking steps to follow the East German lead. Now, the lower West German standard operates in East Germany.

Mothers get six weeks' paid leave before the birth of their babies, and eight weeks afterwards. Previously, it was 20 weeks in East Germany. 'Mother money' is paid to the parent (mother or father) who stays at home to look after the small children. Either the mother or father gets paid leave when the children are ill. Child benefit depends on family income, starting at 50 marks for the first child, and rising to as much as 240 marks for the fourth child. These figures are reduced for high-income families.

In East Germany, child-care was always cheap, costing as little as seven marks a week for a creche and three marks a week for kindergarten. Both

> **Kindergarten**
> Kindergartens were invented in Germany in 1840 by Friedrich Fröbel. The name means 'child garden'. In kindergarten, children can learn measuring while playing with cups and beakers. They can learn about colour by painting. The idea that children could learn through playing was revolutionary at a time when school meant sitting upright in long rows of desks learning things by heart.

crèches and kindergartens were easy to find, and most children went to one.

Unfortunately, the privatization of industry means that many of these child-care facilities no longer exist. This is making it difficult for mothers in East Germany to go on working. In West Germany, day-care has always been a problem as it is expensive and difficult to find. Kindergarten hours rarely fit the adult working day, making life especially difficult for single-parent families. Even so, four out of five pre-school children go to kindergartens.

Unemployment benefit
When a West German loses his or her job, 66 per cent of the previous income is payable for a year, or up to 27 months for older workers. After that, 'unemployment support' is available, which is about fifty per cent of the previous income. Life becomes very difficult for the long-term unemployed. They help make up the numbers of beggars and the half-million homeless people in West Germany.

Until 1990, the East German constitution guaranteed everybody a job. (Being a student or a mother counted as working.) As a result there was virtually no unemployment. Everyone could earn a living wage. In East Germany's new market economy, there is now unemployment, and unemployment insurance is being set up along West German lines. By European standards, this offers reasonably good protection.

Retirement

When people retired in East Germany, the cost of housing was low enough for them to enjoy a good standard of living. This flat is owned by a retired single woman in Dresden.

Men and women retire at the age of 65. In West Germany, pensions depend on the contributions people have made during their working lives. Pensions can be as high as 6000 marks per month, or as low as 600 marks. With low pensions, there are state supplements for rent, heating and

clothing, while TV licences are free.

Before 1990, East Germany guaranteed a minimum pension of 440 marks per month for everyone. Certain people, such as doctors, professors and politicians, could be awarded extra. These figures used to seem low compared with West Germany, but of course housing and power cost much less. Now, East German pensions are earnings-related as in West Germany.

Education

Children begin school at the age of six. Almost all schools are mixed, and there are hardly any private, fee-paying schools. School starts early, and is mainly in the mornings only. Older children usually work a longer school day, on some days as much as nine hours. There is homework as well.

Most schools are in modern buildings. This school at Brunswick has been built among new housing.

West German schools are run by the various state governments, so there can be quite big differences between them. Schools are usually fairly informal, though, with a five-day week. At the age of ten (sometimes 12), children either go to a Junior School for five years, to an Intermediate School for six years, or to a *Gymnasium* for nine years. A Gymnasium is the equivalent of a grammar school or senior high school. Gymnasium students mostly go on to university.

East Germany has had a different system. Children had ten years at a comprehensive, with school on Saturdays. When the children left, many went on to vocational courses. Only about ten per cent of children stayed on the extra two years at school to qualify for university. This is a very low figure for an industrial country, and far behind West Germany's 29 per cent. It is probably one of the reasons why East Germany fell behind in technical development.

10 Everything in order

Alles in Ordnung, 'everything in order', is sometimes used to sum up the way Germans go about things. Germans are often described as hard-working, strict and orderly. As if in revolt, younger Germans in particular, like to appear more relaxed. There is a grain of truth, though, in the idea of German orderliness. It shows in the thorough way businesses are run. However, rather than thinking in terms of a single overall picture, Germans themselves are much more aware of regional differences. They think of themselves as different 'tribes' who have always lived in certain areas. Germans have strong mental pictures of these 'tribes'.

Prussians *(Preussen)*

Prussia was the biggest German state, with Berlin its capital. Of all Germans, perhaps the Prussians were the model for the picture of an orderly people. Prussians seemed never to be 'off duty', even when sitting having a beer. A common motto was *Gemeinnutz vor Eigennutz* – community before self.

Saxons *(Sachsen)*

Saxony is the area around Leipzig. People speak a throaty dialect where, for example, 'k's become 'g's, something which other Germans often find ugly. Saxons filled many official posts over the whole of East Germany, so that Saxons got called 'the fifth occupation army'. The other four refer to the Allies (France, Britain, the US and the USSR) who occupied Germany in 1945. Martin Luther, the playwright Lessing, and the composers Händel, Bach and Wagner, were all Saxons.

Bavarians *(Bayern)*

Bavaria is in the extreme south-east of Germany. With 11 million inhabitants it's the biggest of all the states, bigger than Holland, Belgium and Luxembourg put together. Bavaria is the most Catholic of the German states. Its capital is Munich, and the playwright Bertolt Brecht was born in the nearby town of Augsburg.

Rhinelanders *(Rheinländer)*

In summer, Germans often lunch out of doors. This is a typical restaurant in the Rhineland.

Rhinelanders are 'Sunday children', people born lucky, or so they say. Certainly, there is an easy-going and hospitable feel to life in the Rhinelands,

and the wine is excellent.

Many Rhinelanders have become known internationally. They make an amazing mix, including Karl Marx and Friedrich Engels, the men whose writings inspired socialism and twentieth-century communist revolutions; the Nazi chief, Joseph Göbbels; the writer Heinrich Heine; Röntgen, the inventor of X-rays; and Konrad Adenauer, West Germany's first Chancellor from 1949 to 1963.

Houses and palaces

German houses are traditionally built in distinctive regional styles. In the south, wooden houses are still built in the highly decorated Black Forest style – a style that is immediately familiar to anyone who has seen German cuckoo clocks. In

Plattdeutsch, Hochdeutsch

The German tribes originally spoke different versions of a language called Low German (*Plattdeutsch*). These dialects still survive and people are proud to speak them. Dutch, the language of the Netherlands, is a further variation of Low German. Dutch and Deutsch are really the same word. Some Low German dialects are so different that their speakers cannot understand each other.

Slowly, a form of written German evolved, which could be understood by all the different German tribes. It was particularly helped by Luther's German Bible. The new language became known as High German (*Hochdeutsch*) and educated Germans started speaking it, as well as foreigners. Eventually, it became the national language.

the more mountainous areas, roofs get larger, with a greater overhang to throw off heavy rain and snow. All over Germany, a lot of half-timbered houses still remain. Peasant farms in Lower Saxony were originally made of *Fachwerk*, a timber frame filled in with clay or plaster. When a farmer became wealthy, he would have the filling replaced with stone. So Germans now talk about someone being *steinreich*, stone rich.

Perhaps more than any other country, Germany became a land of palaces and castles. Each prince or duke in the many tiny states had to have his own

Perhaps more than any other country, Germany became a land of palaces and castles. This picturesque little fortress, the Pfalzgrafenstein, is like a little warship afloat on its island in the middle of the Rhine at Kaub. It was originally used to stop boats and collect tolls.

palace. Nineteenth-century businessmen copied the palaces, especially along the banks of the larger rivers such as the Rhine and the Mosel. Their palaces keep alive for tourists the romantic tradition which lives on in German fairy stories and legends.

Most West Germans, however, live in very modern houses or apartments, furnished to a high standard with fitted kitchens and bathrooms. Far more East Germans live in apartments than houses because of government housing policy, but the standard of interior fittings is not far behind West Germany's. Interest-free loans were available to young East German couples setting up home or wishing to restore an old house. How much they paid back depended on the number of children the couple had. However, young couples usually spent several years on a waiting list.

Wurst, Sauerkraut and Knödel

The first German food that people from other countries think of is perhaps sausages and pickled cabbage, *Wurst* and *Sauerkraut*. Germany does indeed specialize in sausages, and it is easy to buy many different kinds, from liver sausage to *Mettwurst*, made with smoked meat and peppercorns. Some shops specialize only in sausages and cooked meat. As well as cabbage, German pickle beetroot, herring, goose and pork. Another typical German food is *Knödel*, or dumplings. These come in many varieties.

German breakfasts seem strange to English, US or Australian tastes. People can start with cereal, of course, but the main part of a German breakfast is black rye bread or some of the many kinds of

Bavarian Farmhouse Dumplings

You need: 6 soft bread rolls, bacon fat, 2 tablespoons chopped parsley, 250 grams (10 oz) plain flour, 250 ml (½ pint) milk, 125 grams (4–6 oz) ham, a pinch of salt.

Cut the rolls into small cubes. Fry them in the bacon fat with the parsley until they are browned.

Mix the flour, salt and milk into a paste and add the bread cubes. Leave for one hour.

Dry your hands with a little flour and roll the mixture into balls 5–8 centimetres (2–3 inches) across. Lower them carefully into boiling water and simmer. When they rise to the surface and turn over, they are ready.

Serve with roast ham. *Guten Appetit!*

The Germans are very fond of sausage or wurst. *There is an enormous variety as this display shows.*

German rolls. With their rolls, people eat jam, or thinly sliced cheese or cold meats. In hotels, there is often a central table for people to help themselves. In some tourist hotels in East Germany, there are even less familiar breakfast foods catering for visitors from eastern Europe or the Soviet Union. From seven in the morning a person can choose kebab, cabbage soup or goulash.

11 Religion, arts and leisure

During the years of division, both German states guaranteed citizens' religious rights. In West Germany, churches have been able to charge their members taxes which are usually collected by state authorities. In East Germany, for 40 years, churches were tolerated rather than welcomed by the government. The Communist party created an alternative to confirmation and communion with a Youth Dedication ceremony. In group meetings, 14-year-olds solemnly promised to abide by the socialist state and its ideals.

The Catholic Church

The Catholic Church has always been strongest in southern Germany, particularly in Bavaria. As a result, the post-war division left East Germany with only six per cent Catholics against 39 per cent Protestants. In West Germany, 45 per cent of the population belongs to the Catholic Church, and 42 per cent to one of the several Protestant churches. Like many other countries today, though, most people prefer sport and recreation on Sunday mornings. In West Germany only about 17 per cent of Catholics and 11 per cent of Protestants are churchgoers.

The Protestant Church

The Protestant Church in East Germany has been not only a place for religion. It has also been a rallying point for people who disagreed with the

Religion has played an important part in Germany's history and almost every village and town is dominated by the tower of a church.

government's policies, but dared not show their views openly. The Church has stood out against violations of human rights and military training in schools, for example. After the fortieth anniversary of East Germany in October 1989, the peaceful demonstrations every Monday evening in Leipzig began with prayers in all the city's churches.

'Church Days' have been growing in importance. These are large-scale forums to debate important issues such as peace and the environment. They have been surprisingly successful throughout Germany, attracting 100 000 or more to the different meetings. Concerned young people outnumber churchgoers and young Communists also attend.

Other religions

Where there were 530 000 Jews living in pre-war Germany, Nazi killings have left only about 35 000, mostly in West Germany. West Germany's use of foreign workers means there is now a significant Greek Orthodox Church. The fastest growth, though, has been of Islam, and there are now 1.8 million Muslims, mainly Turkish, in West Germany.

Music

Germany has a long musical tradition. In the eighteenth-century, Handel and Bach developed courtly music of great elegance. Beethoven's stirring music was influenced by the revolutionary movements of nineteenth-century Europe. Wagner wrote heroic operas, performed in the opera house at Bayreuth, about legendary figures

Germany was the birthplace of some of the world's greatest musicians. In many cities bandstands have been built in the parks, such as this one at Aachen. Regular open-air concerts are held in the summer.

such as Tristan and Isolde, and Lohengrin.

On the whole, German pop groups have not hit the international scene, except perhaps for Nena and Modern Talking from West Germany, and Silly with Tamara Danz from East Germany. There is a strong folk music tradition. Since 1968 there have also been many protest singers, and Wolf Biermann, for example, was forced to leave East Germany in 1977 because of his biting lyrics.

Playwrights

Germany's most famous romantic playwrights were Goethe and Schiller, who worked at Weimar in the late eighteenth and early nineteenth century. They chose large-scale themes, and wrote in verse. Goethe's best-known play is perhaps *Faust*, and Schiller's, *The Robbers*. Later, when opera was usually still concerned with kings and princes, first Georg Büchner and then Gerhard Hauptmann wrote plays about common people. *The Weavers*, a play based on a actual revolt by grossly ill-treated workers, caused an uproar when it was first produced in 1892.

In the early twentieth century, a People's Theatre (the *Volksbühne*) grew up in Berlin, the forerunner of several left-wing or revolutionary theatres. Bertolt Brecht came out of this movement, and his plays such as *Mother Courage* and *The Caucasian Chalk Circle* have become internationally famous.

Playwrights such as Peter Weiss and Rolf Hochhuth have taken up the tradition of political theatre. Others of importance are Botho Strauss and Franz Xaver Krötz in West Germany and Heiner Müller and Peter Hacks in East Berlin.

Philosophers

Germany is famous for its philosophers. Leibniz lived in the seventeenth century, Kant in the eighteenth century and Hegel, Schopenhauer, Marx and Nietzsche in the nineteenth century. Marx developed theories of social revolution which led to the socialist movement and the revolutions in Russia and China. Some of Nietzsche's ideas were taken up by the Nazi movement.

Novelists

Thomas Mann and Herman Hesse, writing in the first half of this century, both won Nobel Prizes. Since the war, the best-known West German authors have been Heinrich Böll, also a Nobel prize-winner, and Günter Grass. Grass's *Tin Drum* creates a vivid picture of Germany through the eyes of a man who has chosen not to grow up. It mixes a dream world with reality to question Nazi values.

In East Germany, the Communist novelist Anna Seghers has been highly influential with novels like *The Seventh Cross*. One disciple, Christa Wolf, has written about Germany's division in *The Divided Sky*. Although socialist, Christa Wolf was nevertheless critical of East German socialism. Stefan Heym was equally critical and his novels, such as *Five Days in June* about the 1953 Berlin uprisings, were published only in West Germany before 1989. When *Five Days in June* was published in East Germany, it was sold out within hours. Many West Germans think that the situation in East Germany gave rise to the more interesting writing.

Arts and the media

The strong medieval woodcuts of Albrecht Dürer were followed by the more humanist Renaissance paintings of Hans Holbein the elder and Hans Holbein the younger. Powerful sympathetic sketches of working people are the lifetime's work of Käthe Kollwitz who died in 1945. Georg Grosz has mocked the rich and powerful in cartoons, and Max Ernst is known for his abstract work.

West Germany produced many talented film directors such as Werner Herzog (*Fitzcarraldo*), Wim Wenders (*Paris, Texas*), Margarethe von Trotta (*Rosa Luxemburg*) and Edgar Reitz (*Heimat*). The film and theatre director, Rainer Werner Fassbinder, made carefully-observed human studies. For example, *Fear Eats the Soul*, which was made in 1973, was about a Turkish guest-worker.

Radio and television in West Germany come from nine regional public corporations. Like the BBC, they are financed by licence fees, and share TV channels One and Three. A special corporation based in Mainz provides Channel Two. Commercial broadcasting has only started since the mid-1980s, the biggest stations being RTL Plus and SAT 1. There are many private radio stations. In East Germany until 1990, there were two TV channels and four radio networks. All were state-run, and have now been turned into public corporations.

East German magazines and newspapers were mostly been run by the Socialist Unity party (SED), at least until 1990. Their main newspaper was *Neues Deutschland* (New Germany). Generally, East German newspapers presented the official image of a state without errors. Naturally, people mistrusted what they read. With the fall of Erich Honecker's government, newspapers have begun to publish the truth.

In West Germany, magazines and newspapers such as the daily *Frankfurter Allgemeine* and the *Süddeutsche Zeitung (South German News)* are run by privately-owned companies. Laws restrict the number of newspapers which a publisher may own, so there is a greater range of views than in England or Australia, for example. Good investigative journalism digs into political and economic secrets.

Leisure, and recreation

In West Germany, all kinds of sports are possible, from alpine and cross-country skiing in the south,

One special form of recreation in Germany is for a family to rent a Schrebergarten. *This is a kind of allotment, and was originally meant to give city-dwellers the chance to grow their own garden produce. Nowadays, many schrebergarten are little paradises, with a carefully furnished summerhouse and beautifully tended flowers.*

to seaside holidays in the north. Lakes have been developed as tourist resorts, with hire boats, water-skiing and wind-surfing. On the whole, though, West Germany's high incomes mean many people take package holidays abroad. In fact. West Germans are Europe's biggest travellers. Caravanning holidays right across Europe are very easy with the motorway network.

East Germans have had fewer holiday facilities, but every summer the Baltic coast used to be packed, especially on the island of Usedom. About 0.5 million went to other socialist countries each year. After travel restrictions were lifted, East German visitors poured into West Germany. One young East German, seeing Hamburg's famous entertainment district, the Reeperbahn, said 'It's like being in a film, one I didn't expect to be in until I was a pensioner.'

In Germany, skiing is both a serious sport and a leisure activity. This cross country ski race is taking place in a forest near Kassel.

Sport

Football is a consuming passion for many Germans. Some of the best-known teams are Dynamo Dresden, Hamburg's SV and Bayern München. In the summer of 1990 West Germany won the World Cup. They had previously won it in 1954 and 1974. Brazil and Italy are the only other countries to have won three times.

Germans hold world records in many sports; cycling, canoeing and the winter sports of bobsleighing and speed skating. In the Olympics their athletes won numerous medals, particularly those from East Germany. The West Germans have excelled at horse riding and have won the Prix de Nations five times.

Michael Gross is a champion swimmer and Boris Becker is internationally known as a tennis star, but more recently, many of the best sports personalities have been women. They range from Steffi Graf, winner of Wimbledon in 1990 to become World Champion, to swimming success Kirstin Otto and the award-winning ice-skater Katarina Witt.

12 Germany and the future

The division between the two German states colours all recent history. It is easy to forget how much both states had in common. There were historical and cultural ties, as well as a shared language and family networks.

Historically, ordinary Germans have rarely had any political control. No sooner had all the minor princes and dukes lost their power, than Bismarck created a strong monarchy in which the Prussian way of doing things required people to show a spirit of respect towards authority. People accepted this, and were obedient to the state. The Weimar Republic should have been a chance for the people to have a say in government but the Republic was too weak to resist Hitler's drive to power and demands for obedience to the state.

Finally, after 1945, democratic systems were imposed by the Allies. Many Germans, though, still wanted their government to be like a father-figure. West Germany's Chancellor Adenauer was just such a person. His party ruled for 20 years. Increasingly, West Germans felt their views were not truly represented. It took the events of 1968 to make people understand that it was possible to influence government.

People in East Germany had an equally strong desire for democracy, but most of them dared not speak openly. Instead, many thousands left the country in the 1950s, and then again in 1989. Both those who left and those who stayed shared the

Germany is starting a new period in its history now that the country is reunited. These young children in Leipzig will no longer be growing up in an entirely socialist atmosphere and will experience many changes.

same feeling about the irritations of daily life and, above all, about the border fence.

Many East Germans demonstrated against those who left, shouting *'Wir bleiben hier'* 'We are staying'. They stayed because they believed in socialism as a principle, but wanted to see East Germany's socialism change. They were tired of the state expecting only obedience. They wanted their vote to be worth something.

When popular demonstrations forced Eric Honecker's government to resign in 1989, a new way of life became possible. People began to talk seriously about unification. However, many people, even non-Communists, did not want a market economy if that meant high prices and unemployment. As the fraudulence of Honecker's government came to light, East Germans increasingly saw uniting with West Germany as a solution to their problems. At the same time, very many continued to leave. East Germany could not afford to loose so many of its workers, nor could West Germany afford to receive them. The interests of both states lay in solving the problem.

One state

Unification has raised fears about a shift in the balance of power in Europe. Until 1990, West Germany belonged to NATO, the North Atlantic Treaty Organization, in which the US is the major partner. East Germany belonged to the Warsaw Pact, dominated by the USSR. Now East Germany has been brought into NATO. At the same time, there are huge changes in the USSR and the other Warsaw Pact states. Until 1989, the division between the two German states marked the division between NATO and the Warsaw Pact, between capitalism and communism. In a few short months all this changed.

The united Germany may play a crucial role in the new Europe which is emerging. The enormous joy when the Berlin Wall came down has been replaced by a more sober mood, as Germans weigh up the complex new situation.

Index